Introduction by W. Terrence Gordon

The original forum for this essay was DÆDALUS: *Journal of the American Academy of Arts and Sciences*, Volume 88, Number 2 (1959), pages 339-348, published jointly by the American Academy of Arts and Sciences and the Wesleyan University Press. Seldom does McLuhan weave a finer tapestry than the one to be found in this text, with its warp of media analysis and woof of language and literature. His signature style, a kaleidoscopic offering of themes, is firmly in place:

1) formal causality is explicitly linked to *form* and to McLuhan's best-known dictum: "[T]he formal causes inherent in ...media operate on the matter of our senses. The effect of media, like their 'message' is really in their form and not in their content;"

2) media analysis is linked to rhetoric: "The oligarchic reign of these figures [of rhetoric] was swiftly liquidated by printing;"

3) the development of nationalism under print is described in fuller detail here than in *Understanding Media*;

4) a one-off application of an illuminating *camera obscura* metaphor is applied to the speed-up effected by print and television media;

5) an important qualifier mediates medium and message: "[T]he medium itself is the *ultimate* message [my emphasis];"

6) a new teaching method required by electric hegemony is evoked: "Reading...will have to be taught as if it is heraldry or some quaint codification of reality."

All such comments are incidental (in the best sense of the word) to the blueprint McLuhan sets out for the educational equivalent of a unified field theory in physics. He begins with the observation that "languages old and new would seem to be for participation rather than for contemplation or for reference and classification." With the tacit imprimatur of specialists in the field, or, at least, apparently without needing to advance his ideas in the face of opposition from their quarter ("My suggestion that we might regard languages on one hand as mass media and on the other hand as macromyths seems obvious to the point of triteness to the structural linguists to whom I have mentioned these approaches") McLuhan virtually weds his definition of myth to the definition of the word as sign, as formulated by the father of modern linguistics, Ferdinand de Saussure: "As a word uttered is an auditory arrest of mental motion, and the phonetic translation of that sound into visual equivalence is a frozen image of the same, is not a myth a means of static abstraction from live process?" From this starting point, McLuhan moves toward his conclusion with its clarion call to media ecology via linguistic means.— WTG

Myth and Mass Media

When an attempt is made to bring the relatively articulated concept of "myth" into the area of "media" — a concept to which surprisingly little attention has been given in the past — it is necessary to reconsider both "myth" and "media" in order to get at relevant data. For example, English is itself a mass medium, as is any language employed by any society. But the general use of the phrase "mass media" would seem to record an unfavorable valuation of new media, especially since the advent of the telegraph, the telephone, moving pictures, radio, and television. These media have had the same kind of drastic effect on language and culture that print had in Europe in the sixteenth century, or that it is now having in other parts of the world.

It might even be well to avoid so highly charged a phrase as "mass media" until a little more thought can be given to the problem. Languages as human artifacts, collective products of human skill and need, can easily be regarded as "mass media," but many find it difficult to consider the newer media deriving from these languages as new "languages." Writing, in its several modes, can be regarded technologically as the development of new languages. For to translate the audible into the visible by phonetic means is to institute a dynamic process that reshapes every aspect of thought, language, and society. To record the extended operation of such a process in a Gorgon or Cadmus myth is to reduce a complex historical affair to an inclusive timeless image. Can we, perhaps, say that in the case of a single word, myth is present as a single snapshot of a complex process, and that in the case of a narrative myth with its peripety, a complex process is recorded in a single inclusive image? The multilayered montage or "transparency," with its abridgement of logical relationships, is as familiar in the cave painting as in cubism.

Oral cultures are simultaneous in their modes of awareness. Today we come to the oral condition again via the electronic media, which abridge space and time and single-plane relationships, returning us to the confrontation of multiple relationships at the same moment.

If a language contrived and used by many people is a mass medium, any one of our new media is in a sense a new language, a new codification of experience collectively achieved by new work habits and inclusive collective awareness. But when such a new codification has reached the technological stage of communicability and repeatability, has it not, like a spoken tongue, also become a macromyth? How much compression of the elements of a process must occur before one can say that they are certainly in mythic form? Are we inclined to insist that myth be a reduction of collective experience to a visual and classifiable form?

Languages old and new, as macromyths, have that relation to words and word-making that characterizes the fullest scope of myth. The collective skills and experience that constitute both spoken languages and such new languages as movies or radio can also be considered with preliterate myths as static models of the universe. But do they not tend, like languages in general, to be dynamic models of the universe in action? As such, languages old and new would seem to be for participation rather than for contemplation or for reference and classification.

Another way of getting at this aspect of languages as macromyths is to say that the medium is the message. Only incidentally, as it were, is such a medium a specialized means of signifying or of reference. And in the long run, for such media or macromyths as the phonetic alphabet, printing, photography, the movie, the telegraph, the telephone, radio, and television, the social action of these forms is also, in the fullest sense, their message or meaning. A language is, on the one hand, little affected by the use individuals make of it; but, on the other hand, it almost entirely patterns the character of what is thought, felt, or said by those using it. And it can be utterly changed by the intrusion of another language, as speech was changed by writing, and radio by television.

Is, then, what concerns us as "myth" today a photograph or "still" shot of a macromyth in action? As a word uttered is an auditory arrest of mental motion, and the phonetic translation of that sound into visual equivalence is a frozen image of the same, is not myth a means of static abstraction from live process? A kind of myth-making process is often associated with Hollywood and with Madison Avenue advertising agencies. So far as advertisements are concerned, they do, in intention at least, strive to comprise in a single image the total social action or process that is imagined as desirable. That is, an advertisement tries both to inform us about, and also to produce in us by anticipation, all the stages of a metamorphosis, private and social. So that whereas a myth might appear as the record of such extended metamorphosis, an advertisement proceeds by anticipation of change, simultaneously anticipating causes with effects and effects with causes. In myth this fusion and telescoping of phases of process becomes a kind of explanation or mode of intelligibility.

What are the myths by which men have recorded the action of new media on their lives? Is there significance in the fact that the Oedipus myth has so far not been found among the preliterate? Is the action of literacy in the shaping of individualism and nationalism also severe on kinship structures? Is the Gorgon myth an account of the effects of literacy in arresting the modes of knowledge? Certainly the Cadmus myth about letters as the dragon's teeth that sprang up armed men is an image of the dynamics of literacy in creating empires. H. A. Innis in his *Empire and Communications* has given us a full exegesis of the Cadmus myth. But the Gorgon myth is in much greater need of exegesis, since it concerns the role of media in learning and knowing. Today, when by means of a computer it is easy to translate a mere blueprint of an unbuilt plane into a wind-tunnel test flight, we find it natural to take all flat data into the domain of depth interpretation. Electronic culture accepts the simultaneous as a reconquest of auditory space. Since the ear picks up sound from all directions at once, thus creating a spherical field of experience, it is natural that electronically moved information should also assume this spherelike pattern. Since the telegraph, then, the forms of Western culture have been strongly shaped by the spherelike pattern that belongs to a field of awareness in which all the elements are practically simultaneous.

It is this instantaneous character of the information field today, inseparable from electronic media, that confers the formal auditory character on the new culture. That is to say, for example, that the newspaper page, since the introduction of the telegraph, has had a formally auditory character and only incidentally a lineal, literary form. Each item makes its own world, unrelated to any other item save by date line. And the assembly of items constitutes a kind of global image in which there is much overlay and montage but little pictorial space or perspective. For electronically moved information, in being simultaneous, assumes the total-field pattern, as in auditory space. And preliterate societies likewise live largely in the auditory or simultaneous mode with an inclusiveness of awareness that increasingly characterizes our electronic age. The traumatic shock of moving from the segmental, lineal space of literacy into the auditory, unified field of electronic information is quite unlike the reverse process. But today, while we are resuming so many of the preliterate modes of awareness, we can at the same time watch many preliterate cultures beginning their tour through the cultural phases of literacy.

The phonetic alphabet, which permits the translation of the audible into the visible, does so by suppression of meaning in the sounds of the letters. This very abstract technology has made possible a continuous one-way conquest of cultures by the Western world that is far from finished. But it would seem that with the commercial use of the telegraph during more than a century we have become accessible to Eastern art and technology as well as to preliterate and auditory cultures in general. At least, let us be prepared to consider carefully the formally auditory character in the telegraph and in subsequent electronic forms of codifying information. For the formal causes inherent in such media operate on the matter of our senses. The effect of media, like their "message," is really in their form and not in their content. And their formal effect is always subliminal so far as our ideas and concepts are concerned.

It is easy to trace some of the effects of phonetic writing since they are coextensive with the most familiar features of the Western world. The phonetically written word, itself an abstract image of a spoken word, permits the prolonged analysis of process but does not greatly encourage the application of knowledge to action beyond the verbal sphere. It is not strange, therefore, that the ancient world should have considered applied knowledge under the mode of rhetoric. For writing made it possible to card-catalogue all the individual postures of mind called the "figures" of rhetoric. And these became available to all students as direct means of control over other minds. The oligarchic reign of these figures was swiftly liquidated by printing, a technique that shifted attention from the audience to the mental state of the individual reader.

Writing has given the means of segmenting many phases of knowing and doing. Applied knowledge by the lineal segmentation of outward motion comes with print, which is itself the first mechanization of an ancient handicraft. And whereas writing had fostered the classification of the arts and sciences in depth, print gave access to the arts and sciences at high speed and on one plane at a time. While manuscript culture required gloss and commentary to extract the various levels of meaning it held for the awareness, because of the very slow reading necessary, print is itself commentary or explanation. The form of print is single-leveled. And the print-reader is greatly disposed to feel that he is sharing the movements of another mind. Print drove people like Montaigne to explore the medium as a new art form providing an elaborate means of self-investigation in the act of learning, as well as self-portraiture and self-expression.

By contrast, today we live in a postliterate and electronic world, in which we seek images of collective postures of mind, even when studying the individual. In some respects, myth was the means of access to such collective postures in the past. But our new technology gives us many new means of access to group-dynamic patterns. Behind us are five centuries during which we have had unexampled access to aspects of private consciousness by means of the printed page. But now anthropology and archaeology give us equal ease of access to group postures and patterns of many cultures, including our own.

Electronic tape permits access to the structure and group dynamics of entire languages. My suggestion that we might regard languages on one hand as mass media and on the other hand as macromyths seems obvious to the point of triteness to the structural linguists to whom I have mentioned these approaches. But it may be useful to point to some of the many nonverbal postures, both individual and public, that accompany changes in the media. That is to say, a new form is usually a cluster of items. For example, in the very first decades of printing at the end of the fifteenth century, people became vividly aware of the camera obscura. The relation of this interest to the new printing process was not noted at the time. Yet printing is itself just such a camera obscura, yielding a private vision of the movements of others. While sitting in the dark, one has in the camera obscura a cinematic presentation of the outside world. And in reading print, the reader acts as a kind of projector of the still shots or printed words, which he can read fast enough to have the feeling of re-creating the movements of another mind. Manuscripts could not be read at a speed sufficient to create the sense of a mind actively engaged in learning and in self-expression. But here, centuries before the movie, is the ultimate magic and myth of the movie in the camera obscura. Perhaps as the camera obscura was the first, the movie is the last phase of print technology.

The movie, which has so little in common with television, may be the last image of the Gutenberg era before it fuses via the telegraph, the telephone, radio, and television, and fades into the new world of auditory space. And as the habits of reading print create intense forms of individualism and nationalism, do not our instantaneous electronic media return us to group dynamics, both in theory and in practice? Is not this shift in media the key to our natural concern with the concept and relevance of myth today?

Printing evoked both individualism and nationalism in the sixteenth century, just as it will do again in India, Africa, China, and Russia. For it demands habits of solitary initiative and attention to exactly repeatable commodities, which are the habits inseparable from industry, and enterprise, production and marketing. Where production precedes literacy, there is no uniform market and no price structure. Industrial production without well-established markets and literacy makes "communism" necessary. Such is the state of our own ignorance of our media that we are surprised to find that radio has very different effects in an oral society than it had in our highly literate culture. In the same way, the "nationalism" of an oral world is structured quite differently from the nationalism of a newly literate society. It would appear that to see one's mother tongue dignified with the precise technology of print releases a new vision of unity and power, which remains a subliminal divisive force in the West even today. Unawareness of the effects of our media these past two thousand years and more would seem to be itself an effect of literacy that James Joyce designated as "ab-ced" or absent-mindedness.

The sentiment of spatial and territorial nationalism that accompanies literacy is also reinforced by the printing press, which provides not only the sentiment but also the centralized bureaucratic instruments of uniform control over wide territories.

Perhaps we tend to define myth in too literary a way, as something that can be verbalized, narrated, and written down. If we can regard all media as myths and as the prolific source of many subordinate myths, why cannot we spot the mythic aspect of the current hula-hoop activity? Here is a myth we are living. Many people have puzzled over the fact that children refuse to roll these hoops on roads or walks. A mere thirty years ago a hoop was for rolling. Today, children reject the lineal use of the hoop in an external space. They use it in a nuclear mode as a means of generating their own space. Here, then, is a live model or drama of the mythic power of the new media to alter sensibility. For this change in child behavior has nothing to do with ideas or programs.

Such a changed attitude to spatial form and presence is as definitive as the change from the photographic to the television image. In his *Prints and Visual Communication* (London: Routledge and Kegan Paul, 1953), William M. Ivins explains how the long process of capturing the external world in the "network of rationality," by the engraver's line and by ever more subtle syntax, finally reached conclusion in the photograph. The photograph is a total statement of the external object without syntax. This kind of peripety will strike the student of media as characteristic of all media development. But in television the striking fact is that the image is defined by light *through*, not by light *on*. It is this fact that separates television from photography and movie, relating it profoundly to stained glass. The spatial sense generated by television experience is utterly unlike that of the movie. And, of course, the difference has nothing to do with the "content" or the programming. Here, as ever, the medium itself is the ultimate message. The child gets such messages, when they are new, much sooner than the adult. For the adult instinctively retards awareness that will disturb a cherished order of perception or of past experience; the child would seem to have no such stake in the past, at least when he is facing new experience.

It is my point that new spatial orientation such as occurs in the format of the press after the advent of the telegraph, the swift disappearance of perspective, is also discernible in the new landscapes of Rimbaud in poetry and Cézanne in painting. And in our time Rouault anticipated the mode of the television image by decades. His use of stained glass as a means of defining the image is what I have in mind.

The mythmaking power of a medium that is itself a myth form appears now in the postliterate age as the rejection of the consumer in favor of the producer. The movie now can be seen as the peak of the consumer-oriented society, being in its form the natural means both of providing and of glorifying consumer goods and attitudes. But in the arts of the past century the swing has been away from packaging for the consumer to providing do-it-yourself kits. The spectator or reader must now be cocreator. Our educational establishment naturally lags behind the popular media in this radical change. The young, when exposed to the television image, receive at once a total orientation in spatial matters that makes the lineality of the printed word a remote and alien language. Reading for them will have to be taught as if it were heraldry or some quaint codification of reality. The assumptions about reading and writing that accompanied the monarchy of print and the related rise of industrial forms are no longer valid for, or acceptable to, those being re-formed in their sensibilities in the electronic age. To ask whether this is a good or a bad thing is to express the bias of efficient causality, which is naturally that of the man of the printed word. But it is also a futile gesture of inadequacy to the real situation. The values of the Gutenberg era cannot be salvaged by those who are as unaware of how they came into existence as they are of why they are now in the process of liquidation.

Philosophic agreement is not necessary among those who are agreed that the insistent operation of media-forms on human sensibility and awareness is an observable, intelligible, and controllable situation. Today, when ordinary consciousness is exposed to the patternmaking of several media at once, we are becoming more attentive to the unique properties of each of the media. We can see both that media are mythic "images" and that they have the power of imposing subliminally, as it were, their own assumptions. They can be viewed at the same time as intelligible explanations of great tracts of time and of the experience of many processes, and they can be used as a means of perpetuating such bias and preference as they codify in their structure.

It is not strange that we should long have been obsessed with the literary and "content" aspect of myth and media. The "form" and "content" dichotomy is as native to the abstract, written, and printed forms of codification as is the "producer" and "consumer" dichotomy.

Unfortunately for the direction and control of education, such a literary bias is quite unable to cope with the new "images" of the postliterate age. As a result of our using literary lenses, the relevant new data have escaped our scrutiny. My book, *The Mechanical Bride: Folklore of Industrial Man*, is a case in point. Turning literary guns on the new iconology of the Madison Avenue world is easy. It is easy to reveal mechanism in a postmechanical era. But I failed at that time to see that we had already passed out of the mechanistic age into the electronic, and that it was this fact that made mechanism both obtrusive and repugnant.

One of the great novelties effected by printing was the creation of a new sense of inner and outer space. We refer to it as the discovery of perspective and the rise of representation in the arts. The space of "perspective" conditioned by an artificially fixed stance for the viewer leads to the enclosing of objects in a pictorial space. Yet so revolutionary and abstract was this new space that poets avoided it in their language for two centuries after painters had accepted it. It is a kind of space very uncongenial to the media of speech and of words. One can gain some idea of the psychic pressures exerted by print in the work of William Blake, who sought new strategies of culture to reintegrate the segmented and fractured human spirit. In fact, the explicit mythmaking of Blake is the greatest monument and antidote to the mythic pressures of the printing press, to "single vision and Newton's sleep." For the matrix of movable type contains the totality of industrialism as well as the means of global conquest, which, by peripety, brought the preliterate world once more into the heart of the industrial metropolis.

The prevalent concept that the mass media exert a baneful influence on the human spirit has strange roots. As Marjorie Nicholson has shown in *Newton Demands the Muse*, it was Newton's *Opticks* that taught poets the correspondence between the inner and outer worlds, between the structure of seeing and the structure of the scene. This notion planted in poets the ambition to gain control over the inner life by a calculus of landscape composition. The idea of verbally constituted landscape, as a lever upon the psychic eye of man, was a dichotomy quite congenial to the culture of the printed word. And whereas external landscape has been abandoned for inner landscape since Rimbaud, Madison Avenue clings to the earlier Romantic concept of consumer control by means of externally arranged scenes. The recent flutter about "subliminal" advertising indicates the delayed shift of attention from outer to inner landscape that occurred in many of the arts in the later nineteenth century. And it is this same shift that today focuses attention on myth in all its modes. For myth is always a montage or transparency comprising several external spaces and times in a single image or situation. Such compression or multilayering is an inescapable mode of the electronic and simultaneous movement of information, whether in popular media or esoteric speculation. It is, therefore, an everyday occurrence for academic entertainment to stress "content," while displaying complete illiteracy with regard to media old and new. For we have now to possess many cultural languages for even the most ordinary daily purposes.

The newspaper will serve as an example of the Babel of myths or languages. When information from every quarter arrived at the same time, the paper became a daily snapshot of the globe, and "perspective" in news became meaningless. Editorials could still try to tie some items together into a chain or sequence with a special point of view or vanishing point. But such views were really capsules for passive readers, while, paradoxically, the unprocessed, uninterpreted, raw news offered far more challenge to the reader to find his own meanings. Today it is easy to see how Edgar Allan Poe, both in his symbolist poems and in his detective stories, had anticipated this new mythic dimension of producer orientation by taking the audience into the creative process itself.

Likewise, it is easy to see how the spot news of the telegraph press really acts like the yes-no, black-white dots of the wirephoto in creating an inclusive world image. Yet even now the sponsors of pre-electronic media continue to overlay the new myth by injections of earlier myth, creating hybrids of the "horseless carriage" variety in the interests of superior culture.

The same type of confusion exists in education in the concept of "audio-visual aids." It would seem that we must do in education what the poets, painters, and composers have done, namely, to purge our media and test and define their unique powers before attempting Wagnerian concerts. The Gutenberg myth was not a means of modifying the Cadmus myth, any more than the Henry Ford myth modified the horse and buggy. Obliteration occurred, as it will with the movie under the impact of television, unless we choose to restrain the operation of form on form by due study and strategy. We now stand at that point with regard to all myth and media. We can, perhaps we *must*, become the masters of cultural and historical alchemy. And to this end we can, I suggest, find means in the study of media as languages and languages as myths. For our experience with the grammar and syntax of languages can be made available for the direction and control of media old and new.

Marshall McLuhan

Myth and Mass Media
Marshall McLuhan - Unbound (18)

ISBN: 1-58423-051-7
Library of Congress Control Number 2005927213

Marshall McLuhan Unbound Project Editors
Eric McLuhan, W. Terrence Gordon

Published in United States in October 2005 by
Gingko Press, Inc.
5768 Paradise Drive, Suite J • Corte Madera, CA 94925
(415) 924-9615 • Fax (415) 924-9608
email: books@gingkopress.com
http://www.gingkopress.com

Design, packaging and production: Die Gestalten Verlag, Berlin
Layout and Typography: onlab, Berlin
Fonts: *Dolly* by Underware, *Bullet* by House Industries
Production: Martin Bretschneider, Vinzenz Geppert
Art direction: Robert Klanten

Made in Germany